To all my unique friends.

Always dream **BIG**!

Published in association with Bear With Us Productions

Carter Chow Chow, The Little Dog Who Dreamed Big

ISBN: 978-1-3999-7868-2

www.justbearwithus.com

CARTER CHOW CHOW

The Little Dog Who Dreamed BIG

Written by
Carl Cunard

Illustrated by
Karn Parkrada

WELCOME
TO
ESSEX

In the sunny county of Essex, England,
a **playful doggie called Carter**
lived with his **daddy Carl**.

Carter loved looking at content on **Insta-Woof**, a platform where dogs could post **make-up tutorials**, pose in **fashionable clothes** and perform funny, well-rehearsed **dance videos**.

Carter hoped that one day he would be on Insta-Woof too...

but what content could he possibly post that hadn't already been done?

Carter realised something – none of the Insta-Woof stars looked like him, **he was different**.

He sighed.

The dogs in the park never looked like him either. They never stopped to play with him. If he couldn't even make friends in the park, how could he be on Insta-Woof?

He asked his daddy, “Why am I **different** to the other dogs?”

His daddy explained, “It’s because you’re a **Chow Chow**, which is a **VERY** unusual, special dog breed.”

His daddy helped Carter to **brush his hair**, so it was well-groomed and shiny.

Then they took selfies, pulling **funny faces**.

"See? Looking different can be **fun**!" said Daddy.

Carter felt a lot better about himself.

He felt proud.

After having a morning of fun and laughter,

they decided to take a walk in the park.

"Oh my word, **who is that?**"

"**It's a lion**, isn't it?
Shouldn't they be in the zoo?"

"Nah, it doesn't look like a lion,
it must be a **polar bear.**"

"Shush, shush, **he is coming** this
way, let's go and meet him!"

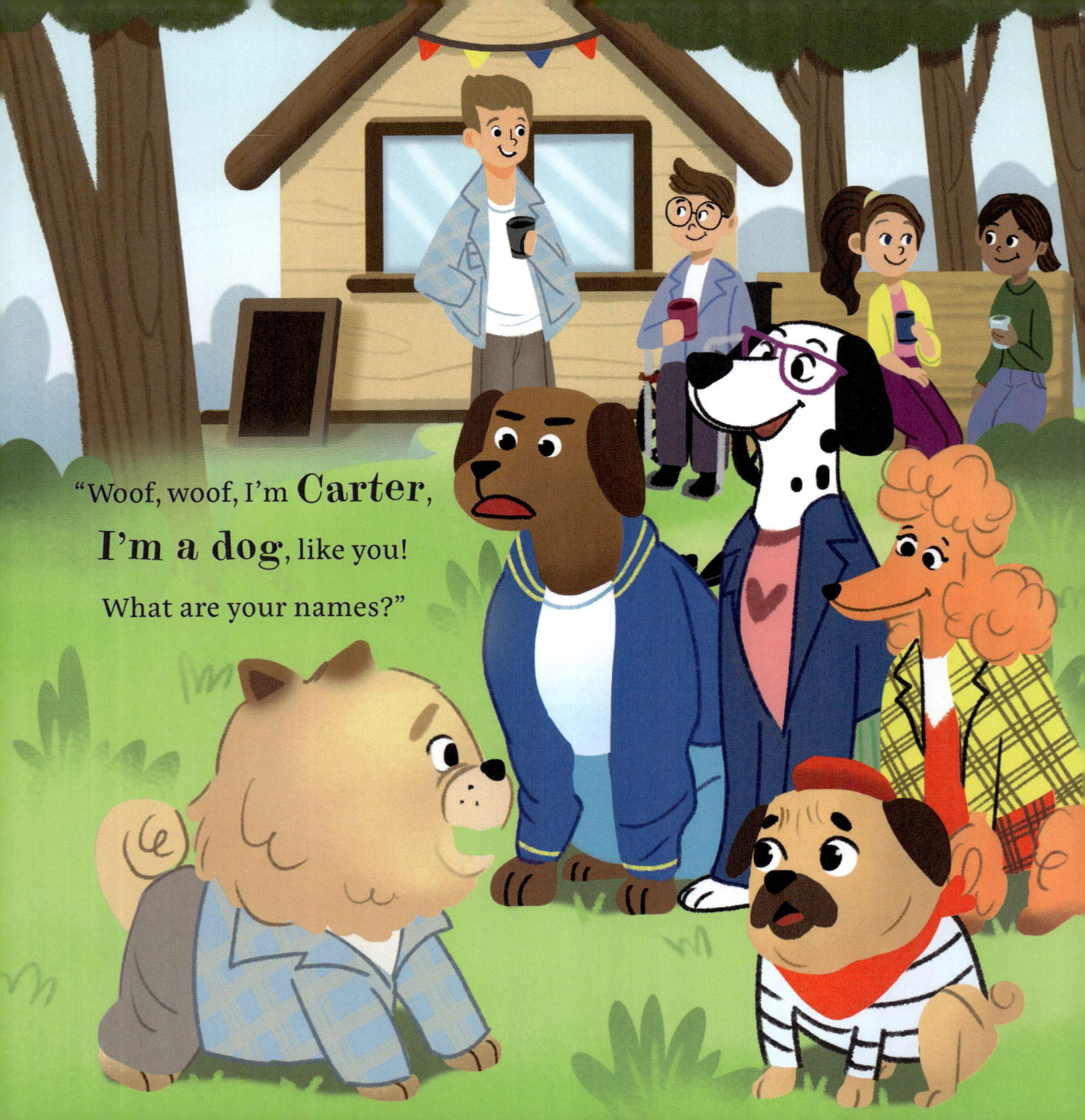

"Woof, woof, I'm **Carter**,
I'm a dog, like you!
What are your names?"

There was...

Pascal the Pug

Penelope the Poodle

Larry the Labrador

Dixie the Dalmatian.

"You don't **LOOK** like a dog to us!"

"That's because I'm a Chow-Chow, I'm **unusual**."

"Wow, I've never heard of a Chow Chow!"

Before long, Carter told them all about his dream to be on Insta-Woof.

“What dreams do you have?” yapped Carter.

Dixie had a puzzled look on her face.

"I think we are just meant

to be dogs, aren't we?"

Carter chuckled to himself,

"NO, NO, NO!

You can be anything you want to

be, if you put your mind to it."

Pascal nervously whimpered,

"Can I be a chef?"

Larry barked with excitement,

"Can I be a firefighter?"

Penelope wagged her well groomed tail and asked,

"Can I be a scientist?"

And finally, Dixie looked up at the sky

and yelped, "Does that mean

I can be a pilot?"

"Yes, of course you can!" bellowed Carter.

The dogs all started to bound about with excitement, buzzing with ideas for ways they could fulfil their dreams.

"**Thank you**, Carter, for telling us about you and your dreams. I felt a bit afraid of you because you didn't look like a dog, I didn't really understand you. I'm glad we're friends now!

Let's play again soon!"

As Carter walked home, feeling confident in himself after the chat with his new friends, he had a **great idea**. If he could help the dogs in the park understand who he was and about what made him different, maybe he could help even **MORE** dogs...

Carter decided now was the time to

follow his dream

and start an Insta-Woof account!

Once home, instead of putting on make-up or wearing a **special outfit**, Carter recorded **his first video completely unfiltered**, being **honest** about himself.

I'm Carter, a Chow Chow from England, but my family origins are in China, which is very, very far away.

“I have a face
like a furry **lion**,

a black tongue like
a tall **giraffe**

and paws like a **bear.**"

“I hope other dogs who are watching,

who also look different,

can feel **confident** too!

If you see an **unusual dog**, **ask them to play**

instead of growling at them!

You might just make a **friend for life**.”

“So this is the **real me**, 100% unfiltered!”

56
INSTAWOOF
CARTER
27683 LIKES
COMMENTS

Carter received so much **love** and **support**,
with many dogs praising him for his **authenticity** and **honesty**.
They also **shared stories** about their own personal insecurities.

He couldn't wait to share the news

with **Pascal**, **Larry**, **Penelope** and **Dixie**.

As he bounced to the park with a spring in his step,
his new friends came charging towards him, **tails wagging**,
ears flapping and smiling from **cheek to cheek**.

"You did it!" yelped Pascal.

"We saw your post and we are so proud of you!"

"I've been going to the gym to get fit,"

said Larry, demonstrating his Downward Dog pose.

"I've been practicing new recipes,"

barked Pascal, showing off his new chef's hat.

"I've been doing science experiments,"

howled Penelope, parading her new lab coat and safety goggles.

"I've been making my own model planes,"

Dixie said, waving her latest creation around from left to right.

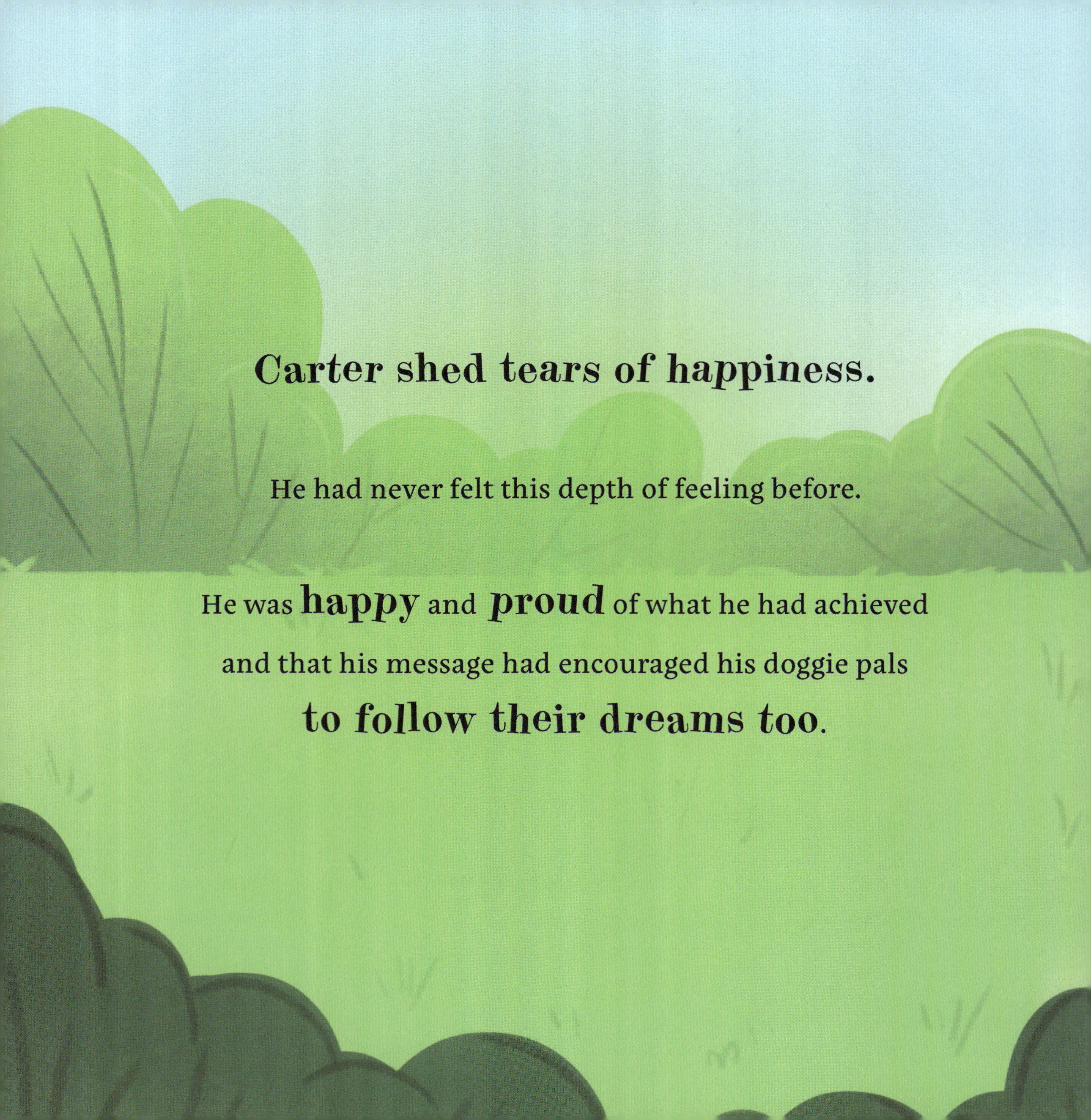

Carter shed tears of happiness.

He had never felt this depth of feeling before.

He was **happy** and **proud** of what he had achieved
and that his message had encouraged his doggie pals
to follow their dreams too.

Carter snuffled whilst pawing away his tears.

“YES, YES, YES!

I can’t wait to see what the **future** holds for us all now!”

FIRE STATION

Printed in Great Britain
by Amazon

60535782R00022